I spy activity coloring book for kids and children Beautiful I spy image to design

This coloring book
is belongs to

....

....

....

FIND TWO SAME CROWNS

WHO IS HIDING IN DISGUISE?
CAN YOU FIND THE REAL COW?

BIRTHDAY PARTY
WORDSCRAMBLE
LOONBAL
LANDEC
FETTICON
I SPY
HOW MANY CAKES?
SPOT 5 DIFFERENCES
PRESENT
CRACKER
CAKE
BALLOON
CANDLE
P R E S E N
C R A C K T
C A K E E R T
C B A A R T
A P L L O Y
N D L E O N

I SPY

I SPY

PUZZLE TIME
I SPY

FIND TWO SAME CROWNS

I Spy

I SPY
PUZZLE TIME

FIND TWO SAME MAGIC CREATURES

ON THE FARM
SPOT 5 MILK BOTTLES
I spy
SPOT 5 DIFFERENCES
1 pink
2 orange
3 green
4 black

I Spy

CAMPING ACTIVITY MAT
FIND 15 MATCHES
I spy
WORDSCRAMBLE
RIFE
PASSMOC
PACKBACK
BIKE
FIRE
GUITAR
COMPASS
ROD
MAP
BACKPACK
BOAT
C O M P A S S
B G U I T A R
A I B F S R B
M N K I R O O
B A S E E D A
A E P O S B T
C K P A C K D

CIRCUS
CONNECT
THE
LETTERS
What numbers
are missing?
HOW MANY
DOVES CAN
YOU SPOT?
I spy
WORDSCRAMBLE
REAB
VEOD
PHANTELE
SPOT 5 DIFFERENCES
1 blue
2 green
3 red
4 yellow
5 grey

Magic Kingdom

BACK TO SCHOOL
2+2=   2+3=
2+4=
I spy
FIND 10 PENCILS
PENCIL
BELL
TEACHER
GLOBE
BOOK
SCHOOLBAG
LAPTOP
PEN
S C H O O L B
B T E A C H A
E G P E N E G
L L L A C R B
L A E O I L O
P P T O B T O
E N B P H E K

FIND AND CIRCLE 2 GROUPS OF OBJECTS

I SPY

HALLOWEEN I SPY

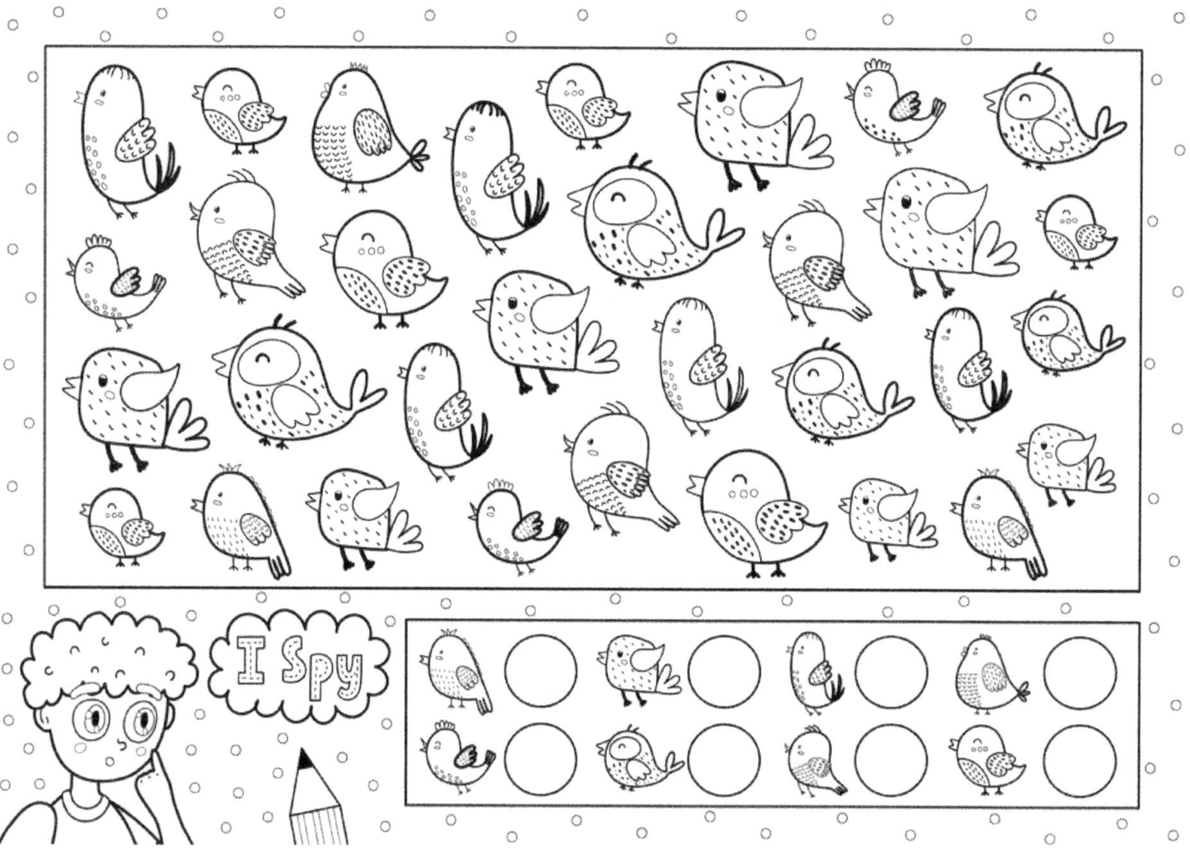

I Spy

I SPY

ON THE FARM
SPOT 10 BELLS
I spy
Find objects in the puzzle
BARN
COW
FARMER
FIELD
GOAT
HEN
PIG
TRACTOR
T R A B A R
C G C F A N
O O T O R M
W A T R H E
P I G D E R
F I E L N B
WORDSCRAMBLE
CWO
TOAG
PHESE
SPOT 5 DIFFERENCES

FIND TWO SAME TURKEYS

I SPY

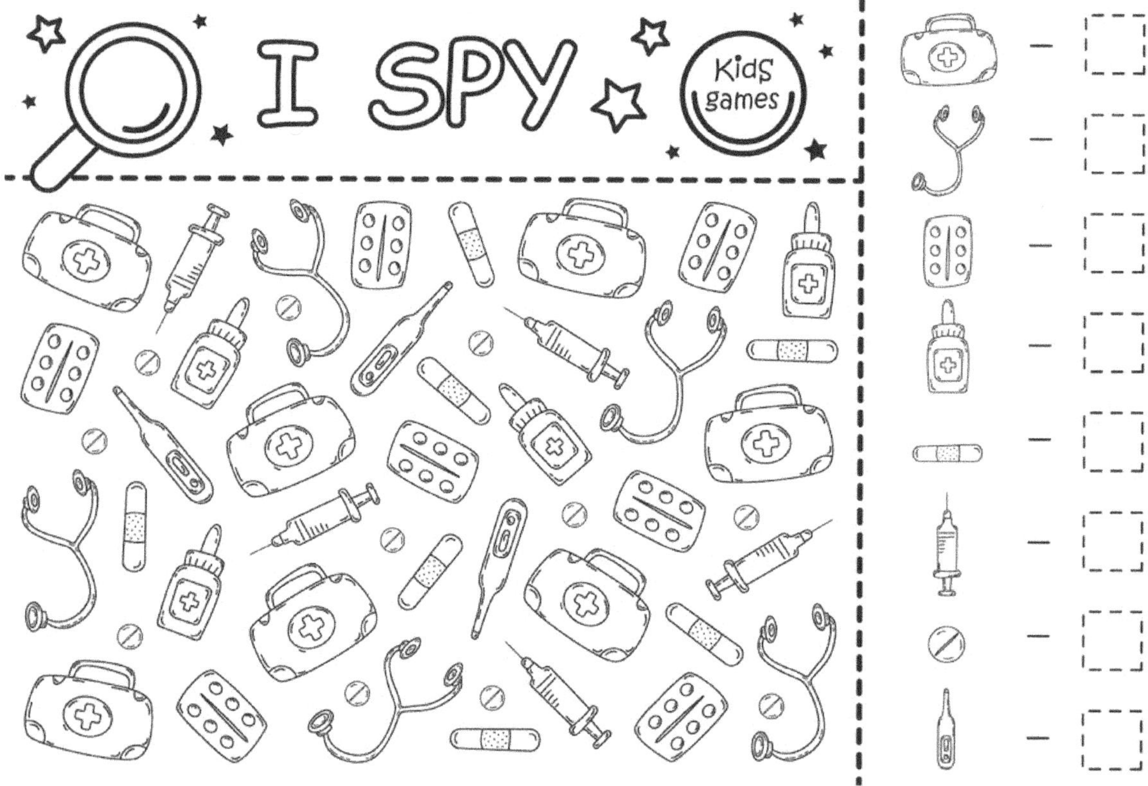

I SPY
Kids
games

I SPY

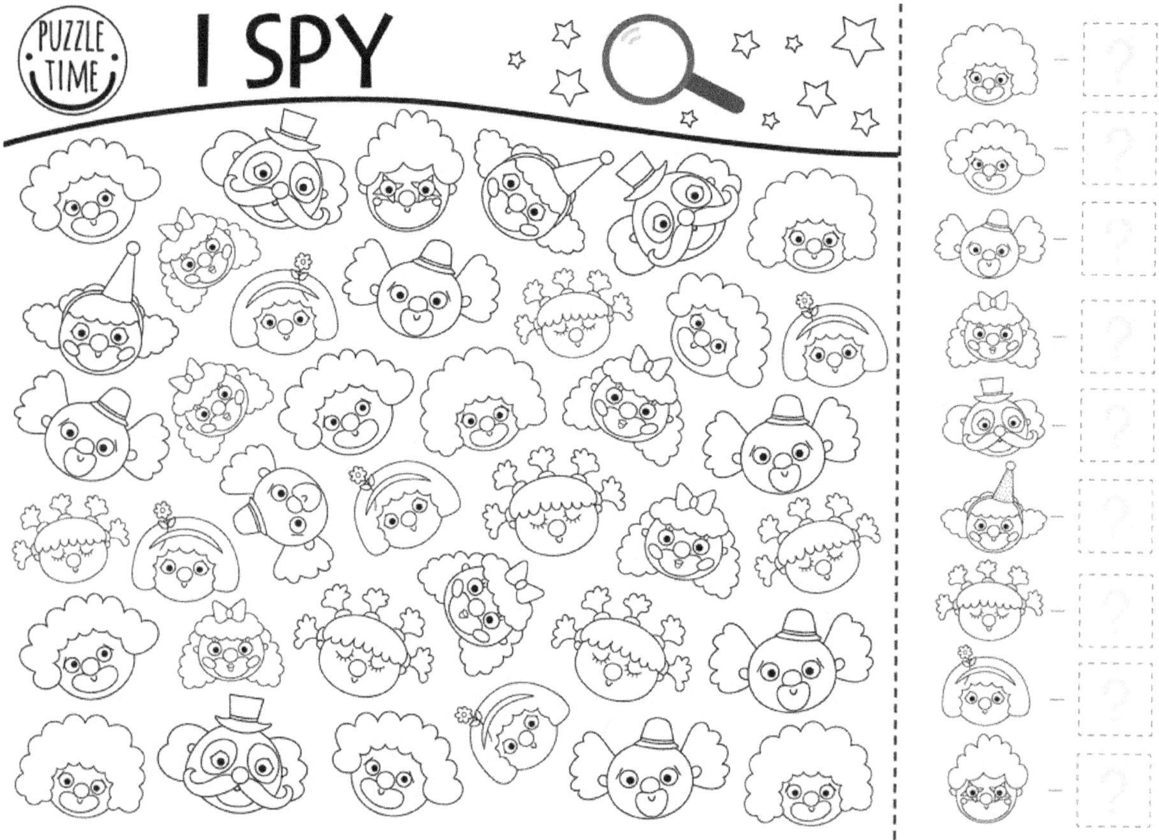

FIND TWO SAME FARMERS

I SPY GAME

FIND AND CIRCLE 2 GROUPS OF OBJECTS

Find the ten differences between the two pictures.

FIND TWO SAME ANIMALS

HELP THE PRINCESS FIND SIX PAIRS OF SHOES

I SPY

I SPY Easter